of Southeast Alaska

Mary Ida Henrikson has made a great contribution to increasing our knowledge of Southeast Alaska Natives' use of the environment through her work culminating in this publication, The Mystery of the Fire Trees of Southeast Alaska. *Although a number of people have been aware of the ancient trees that the Tlingit used as a source to start fires, the extent of fire trees throughout the region and their other possible uses have not been previously recorded. Most often the ethno-archaeological investigations in Southeast Alaska have been conducted in the coastal regions and scientists have rarely ventured far into the forests. Once Mary heard about the fire trees, her natural curiosity and her love of wandering through the woods led to her serious investigation. Her artistic creativity also led her to record the scenes and even take artistic liberty in recording and further elaborating or imagining what the image might have been. Hopefully, her work might spur serious scientific investigation to further validate the role of fire trees and the changes through time.*

— **Rosita K̲aaháni Worl, Ph.D.**
President, Sealaska Heritage Institute
Member of the Tlingit Shangukeidí Clan and
House Lowered from the Sun

There are some fascinating original information and interpretations in the text. Some are very believable, while others strike me as being highly improbable speculations. I think the idea of fire trees as shelter, warmth, and protection for a hearth (as depicted in a sketch) makes a lot of sense. When John Muir traveled with Tlingits in canoes, he camped with open fires on the beach at night. Tlingits guiding him stated they did not traditionally travel that way as smoke and light would expose position and make them vulnerable to possible ambush. I have found campsites on terraces above well-traveled beaches that appear to be located to prevent light and smoke from fire being seen. Fire trees would be a perfect solution to this dilemma—and it makes good sense to me.

"Fire storage" referencing actual fire does not seem plausible. However, during a recent visit to Stanley Park in Vancouver, British Columbia, I saw the "Hollow Tree," a 1,000-year-old red cedar that showed clear and substantial evidence of burning through the enormous amount of charcoal apparent. The substantial charcoal remains in the tree suggested to me that the concept of "fire trees" may reference the creation and utilization of charcoal, an easily ignitable material that would be easily accessible.

— **Stephen J. Langdon, Ph.D.**
Professor Emeritus, Department of Anthropology,
University of Alaska Anchorage

I'm glad to see Mary Ida Henrikson has captured the burned-out cedar trees. They seem to be everywhere when you start looking. It has become a hobby of mine looking for them while walking the Southeast shorelines. I often wonder if there is much really known about them or their true ages. It seems you never hear many people talk of them as time goes on.

— **Dennis Diamond**
Civilian lighthouse technician for U.S. Coast Guard and boatbuilder

Mary Henrikson has pulled together some fascinating material regarding the mystery of the fire trees. There are many stories told by the Tlingit, Haida, and Tsimshian that provide a window into their relationships with the forest and specific trees. Mary's work is an important contribution to the exploration of the interaction between the peoples of Southeast Alaska and their natural world of forest and oceans.

> **— Priscilla Schulte Ph.D.**
> Campus Director and Professor of Anthropology
> University of Alaska Southeast Ketchikan Campus

Mary Henrikson's process combines artistry, science, ethnographic research and direct experience in a way that weaves together the best of each modality. She provides a landscape for exploration, living closely to the land and its people, and gives a powerful and fascinating perspective that could not be accessed by most researchers. She shows us a powerful way of combining methodology and personal insights, bringing the world alive for those who join her.

I have spent hours in discussion with Mary, and each time leave inspired, fascinated and motivated to dive into the mysteries of this world. I believe that by reading this book, you will as well. For in truth, there is so much we don't know, so much that we have lost of old ways and so much to explore. For that, I have always been grateful for the kindred soul I find in Mary. Fire Trees *represents a lifetime of collective experience that culminated in this project of unbounded creativity and provides a model of process for artists, academics and anyone who wants to have a deeper connection to the world around us.*

> **— Joshua Cogan**
> Emmy-winning photographer and anthropologist

Mary Henrikson and I met on the navigation bridge of a ship. I was a newly hired deck officer for the Alaska Marine Highway and she was a senior crew member who came up to "check out the new guy." Mary was one of a collection of experienced shipmates, who were to become my informal tutors of "local knowledge." These knowledgeable Southeasterners had been raised fishing and sailing the waters of Southeast Alaska, and though I had the technical training in modern navigation, they had the hard-won understanding of their surroundings.

The local knowledge they passed on revealed their acute awareness of the marine environment of the Inside Passage: the local weather, tides and currents, and the geography crucial for subsistence, safety, and even survival. Over the length of my maritime career in Southeast Alaska, their teachings have served me well. So, when Mary describes the "black waters of winter," or how a navigation light is "as precious, as it is a precaution" she knows of which she speaks.

Her work correlating visual landmarks used for water travel with fire trees as navigational aids is extremely credible. The fire trees on Betton Island were perfectly located, and oriented, to have guided Native canoeists from the exposed waters of Clarence Strait to the safety of port. The tree on Gravina Island was very well-positioned to have served as a homing beacon for travelers on the long water journey from Haida Gwaii, across the unprotected, dangerous waters of Dixon Entrance.

If I were alone in a canoe on the "black waters" of Southeast Alaska, I would not only welcome the reassuring light of a fire tree, I would consider it essential to my survival. I believe Mary Henrikson has rightly revealed fire trees as prehistoric navigational aids of the indigenous peoples of Southeast Alaska.

    *— **Captain Jeff Baken***
    Southeast Alaska Pilots' Association

The Mystery
of the Fire Trees
# of Southeast Alaska

Mary Ida Henrikson

VII

SEVENTH GENERATION ARTS

MaryIdaHenrikson.com

Copyright © Mary Ida Henrikson

Seventh Generation Arts
P.O.B. 998   Ward Cove, Alaska   99928
www.maryidahenrikson.com

All rights reserved. No part of this publication may be reproduced, sorted in a retrieval system, or transmitted in any form or by any means electronic, mechanical, photocopying, recording, or otherwise, without the prior written permission of the publisher. Permission is given for brief excerpts to be published with book reviews in newspapers, magazines, newsletters, catalogs, and online publications. Trademarks are used in the text of this book only for informational purposes and no affiliation with or endorsement by the trademark owners is claimed or supported.

Painting on front cover by Mary Ida Henrikson
Photo on back cover by Mary Ida Henrikson

Photographs, illustrations and paintings inside the book
by Mary Ida Henrikson except as noted in captions

Design by Gregg Poppen
Maps by Gregg Poppen & Terry Pyles

Printed in the U.S.A.

ISBN 978-1-935347-08-8 paperback

ISBN978-1-945347-76-7 Ebook

DEDICATION

To my late sister, Nancy Henrikson DeWitt ... an artist, illustrator and master gardener who taught me to be brave and curious as she dragged me on adventures, and who was a naturalist by training and acute observation. If not for her, I wonder, who would I be?

Contents

Foreword ... xiii

Introduction ... xvii
Seeking Secrets from a Wonderful Past

Chapter One ... 1
One of Those Trees

Chapter Two ... 5
Fire Storage

Chapter Three ... 13
The Art of Investigating Fire Trees

Chapter Four ... 23
Lighthouses and Signal Trees

Chapter Five ... 30
Settlers Cove State Park

Chapter Six ... 39
Maps, Charts and Point of View

Chapter Seven ... 49
Cooking and Life Celebrations

Chapter Eight ... 52
Fire Trees Today

Chapter Nine ... 55
Others Join the Search

Conclusion ... 59
So Many Trees, So Little Time

Epilogue ... 62
The Great Hollow Cedar

Bibliography ... 64

Acknowledgments ... 65

This ancient vestige of Northwest Coast Natives' fire trees stands in Stanley Park in Vancouver, British Columbia.

FOREWORD

Mary Henrikson and I have shared concepts and observations on the lush rainforests of Southeastern Alaska for many years. During one of our discussions, she mentioned the ancient fire trees, wondering if I had seen any. I had, near where one might camp today, but I was not paying great attention to their function other than as a source of dry fine tinder if needed.

After our talk evolved into the possible function of fire trees as "lighthouses" used by early Southeastern Natives for communication, I began paying closer attention to their position and individual nuances. Other researchers and friends were brought into the search.

These fascinating trees generally have hollow, burnt center cores encased in live red cedars. Their importance and role in Native life have been lost with those who created them. I now believe that some were places to ensure dry, fire-starting tinder. Some may have been created while searching for trees appropriate for canoes or other projects.

Some, however, seem to be strategically located and designed as beacons across channels or on points of land near

xiii

historic Tlingit, Haida and Tsimshian villages.

Many have back doors to feed or vent the fires, seen only through crafted, focused openings on the opposite side. These most certainly could have been created as a way to communicate from one village to another or to guide home those upon the sea.

The fire trees that survive today were generally used or created before contact with European and Russian explorers in the mid- to late 1700s. With a life expectancy of five hundred to seven hundred years, some of these red cedar fire trees may have been created between 1400-1800 A.D. Shorelines change. People's use of patterns on the landscape changes. So do cultures.

Southeast Alaska holds many secrets in its mist-shrouded islands. Our understanding of the past is imperfect. Mary's art and storytelling here focus on one small but fascinating aspect of that past, introducing the reader to the possible uses and importance of the fire trees, creating images that span functionality and spirituality. This collection of stories and images beckons others to study further, to be aware of the possibilities, to more fully make the connection between the land and its inhabitants.

Mary Henrikson is a true Alaskan. Born and raised in the dynamic landscape called Southeast, she has lived remotely both there and in the Interior of this great state. Through family and friends, she has experienced Native traditions and spirituality that have greatly influenced her art and perceptions of the natural world. Mary's fascinating inquisitiveness drives her insatiable quest to learn.

Foreword

I am the geologist for the Tongass National Forest. My work centers on the geology and glacial history of this great land. Most recently I have been focusing on how the glaciers influenced the stand of the sea through time—important if you want to know where early inhabitants camped and subsisted. It's a puzzle, just like the mystery of the fire trees, which Mary Henrikson may well have figured out.

Jim Baichtal
Forest Geologist
Tongass National Forest
U.S. Forest Service
September 3, 2016

"*A dying cedar, its naked, grey wood without live branches: a cedar snag shaped like a totem, facing the sun and greeting the new day. I never forgot my curiosity about that tree.*"

INTRODUCTION

Seeking Secrets from a Wonderful Past

When I was a child in Ketchikan, I would wake in the early hours of Southeastern Alaska's sunny summer mornings and look at a mountain ridge, drawing with my eyes the outlines of the trees against the blue sky. On one ridge was a dying cedar, its naked, grey wood without live branches: a cedar snag shaped like a totem, facing the sun and greeting the day. I never forgot my curiosity about that tree.

I don't remember ever walking through the woods as a child. I was always running: alone, with my sister, or with friends. The forest was our playground, complete with forts, hideouts, and swings. I made my first ascent on a huge old-growth cedar that had a split top filled with years of plant debris. When our parents came looking for us, we could hide on its natural platform, knowing they would never look up. There was another huge cedar with a high root and deep dropoff where an accommodating branch could be pulled back, swung upon, and we could drop and roll down the moss.

I remember the first time I heard the wind in the trees. I was a teenager. The song was always there, but one day I realized what made the music. That kind of untutored revelation is powerful.

Our home was next to a deep canyon cut by a creek large enough to supply electricity from its head waters at Carlanna Lake. Part of our playground was a tangle of animal trails down a steep cliff, where we could hang from roots with our eyes on the goal: that wondrous creek with round rocks and stepping stones. We built dams to make swimming holes and looked for gold, believing that finding mica—"fool's gold"—was just as good. We also walked upstream past our boundaries to a cave that our parents had been wise enough to warn us was occupied by the ghosts of gold miners. We would stare into that abyss with frightened wonder.

The lush, green rain forest of Southeastern Alaska and its rich heritage continue to fascinate me. The Tlingit, Haida, and Tsimshians, who lived here before Western explorers arrived, thrived on these generous shores. This was the knowledge the Natives of Southeastern Alaska owned, just as much as they owned the resources upon which they relied, such as king salmon runs, obsidian mines, straight-grained cedar groves, and fish-processing sites. Throughout the region, they were rich in art and culture, developing a sophisticated society. They had a talent for assimilating other cultures, and could focus on the future without abandoning ancient beliefs and practices.

Dwelling on Southeastern Alaskan shores for thousands

of years, the ancestors of these tribes populated the coast at the end of the last Ice Age, and they continue to succeed in the twenty-first century. I had access to their cultures growing up in Ketchikan, where I lived in their realm, and I still maintain a remote cabin surrounded by the trees that are part of my own heritage.

In the Tongass, the vast 16.8-million-acre forest of the Southeastern region, one easily steps from the beach into the mysterious woods, and there is always a surprise. When I was young, I would lay my head on the mossy forest floor, focus on the tiny fungi and flowers, and pretend it was a fairyland as the pinks and greens became pathways into my imagination. I picked berries and gathered mushrooms, edible greens, raw material for remedies and tea as good as any Asian black tea. Later in life, I found a grotto with a heavenly moss carpet dotted with tiny orchids, and a small salmon stream with aged, blown-down trees perfectly positioned as bridges between the streambanks. I learned that one cannot transplant the tiny orchids because the microenvironment is so specialized. I found a cliff near a beach of quartz crystals on a magic island near Kuiu Island that I do not care to name; at the base was a wide animal trail, and again there was inviting moss covered with tiny, wild blossoms. The Tongass is a matrix where wonders lead to wonders.

When I was young, I discovered a charred chamber inside a tall red cedar, where it was impossible to resist entering and looking out the entrance at yet another vista, another point of view. Yet, perhaps because the whole forest is so mysterious, I failed to question or wonder about the singular origins of that burned relic. And in the decades to follow—beachcombing, living remotely, and walking animal trails—I never really thought about other burned cedar chambers. Lightning strikes, I casually assumed—just lightning striking the cedars.

So, late in life, when a friend told me the Natives had stored their fire in those burned-out trees, I was surprised. I had never heard of "fire trees" in my decades of living here. I had not found a single reference in academic literature or in any nineteenth-century text. Was this something the anthropologists had missed?

Fire trees! *Fire trees*? I decided their unique development was a convenience, like running water and indoor plumbing. I needed to know more. I studied the old with a new appreciation—not as a scientist, but as an artist, for that is what I am trained to be.

This creative approach does not preclude logic. If one lives where it is cold and wet, one would want access to warm and dry. I had always imagined people rubbing two sticks together or carrying special kits with flint and tinder, but a whole village's utilizing a fire tree shows sophistication well beyond the flint-and-tinder stage of technological development.

Very soon in the course of my exploration, I came to realize that some of the altered cedars were conveniently located above protected beaches, while others sat on the tops of islands along the nearly five hundred miles of the Alexander Archipelago that makes up the Tongass National Forest. Because of time I had spent rowing a skiff, beachcombing and watching the coastline slip by silently, I noted that many of these trees would have made excellent lighthouses.

Luckily, when I began this study in 2000, there were still Native elders who could confirm some of my hunches, and

Seeking Secrets from a Wonderful Past

my drawings and paintings imagining the use of fire trees helped to fill the gaps. Please explore this unusual world with me to appreciate the sophistication of an ancient culture, once deemed primitive, that was actually well ahead of its time.

Mary Ida Henrikson
Ketchikan, Alaska
February 23, 2015

❝ *Oh, you've got one of those trees.* ❞

CHAPTER ONE

One of Those Trees

At the turn of this century, Captain Lawrence "Snapper" Carson of Ketchikan, Alaska, was towing a bundle of cedar siding from his sawmill to my cabin in Clover Passage, north of Knudson Cove, in Ketchikan. Snapper mills timber from beach logs using a salvage permit issued by the U.S. Forest Service. He also takes logs culled from commercial rafts that break up in storms and drift in to shore. I rode with him as his boat made its unhurried voyage.

Snapper has a heavy-duty aluminum work skiff, much better for towing than my lightweight skiff. Once under way, he told me that going slow is best for studying the shoreline, the best way to notice differences and changes. This was true wisdom, especially from a mariner who piloted packers and slow-moving tugs all over Southeastern Alaska, often running the same course. That's how he spotted the tree that would take me on this journey that you are sharing.

Fire Trees

We were working the tides, arriving at high slack to ensure the lumber could be left high up the beach: easier for me to carry it to the building site. We secured the load, anchored the boat on the outhaul and walked into the woods.

"Oh, you've got one of those trees," he said.

The tree to which he referred was a huge, burned-out red cedar common on the shores of Southeastern Alaska. *Doesn't everyone?* I thought, but I asked him what he meant.

"That's where the Natives stored their fire," Snapper said.

Despite the decades I'd lived in Alaska, this was news to me. I had always thought that these trees were altered by lightning strikes or by kids with matches. However, lightning hits the top of a tree, and mine was burned at the bottom. I never knew anyone who set a tree on fire, nor did I have a desire to do so when I was a child. In fact, it never occurred to me to burn a living cedar purposefully for any reason.

Later, I mentioned this conversation to Dorney Mullins, a retired submariner and merchant seaman. "You won't believe what Snapper told me," I said. But after listening, he described three fire trees next to each other, 180 feet uphill from a beach that overlooks Dixon Entrance near British Columbia, Canada. Mullins said the openings face three different directions.

Lighthouses, I thought.

So began my five-year journey into the Tongass, the largest national forest in America. I saw the forest from a completely new perspective, redefining my appreciation of the great cedars within, and with added appreciation of the ancient culture that thrived around the forest.

The Tongass is host to both red and yellow cedar, and to a dwarf species high in the alpine forest. All the fire trees that

Fire scale—The author's niece, Jami Lee DeWitt, stands in a fire tree to provide a visual reference of the massive size of the red cedar trees used long ago by Alaska Natives.

Fire Trees

I have seen are red cedars. Yellow cedar is an oily tree that burns hot and fast, and pops as it burns, sparks flying. I've heard the expression, "You talk too much; you sound like yellow cedar," as a description of yellow cedar's combustible nature. Yellow cedar is a beautiful, buttery-colored wood that yields durable planks, siding and building uprights. It is also used traditionally for carving and creating storage boxes.

The two kinds of cedar look different from one another, too. The bark on each is a different color, the branches sweep differently, and the withes—small, flexible branches—project at different angles. Author Margaret E. Bell once told me, "Yellow cedar keep their arms close, elbows bent and swept up, while red cedar spread their arms gracefully."

Many of the sites I visited during the early days of my research were private and others were culturally sensitive. I delayed writing about the subject until I found a stand of trees at present-day Settlers Cove State Park in Ketchikan, a site where, I believe, Alaska Natives long ago used cedars for fire storage, navigation, and other purposes that might surprise those unfamiliar with the complexity of their lives.

The state park site of today includes trails, bridges, and even a sign that led the way: *Hollow Cedar Beach Access Trail*.

This marked the official start of my quest.

CHAPTER TWO

Fire Storage

Boredom can creep into a person's life like the aliens in that old sci-fi movie, *Invasion of the Body Snatchers*. Boredom can make a person think the slinky, creeping feeling under one's skin is normal. I am an artist, and I was so bored at the end of the last century that not even a three-season gold mining stretch and a *plein air* painting jaunt into eastern Alaska, enjoying the French idea of painting directly from nature in the good fresh air, could stir my soul. I was determined to quit painting, an art that had been part of my life since I was fourteen. What does one call oneself when one stops being who she is?

Then came the lumber procurement from Snapper and his account of early Alaska Native fire storage.

It was George Eton, who fished and processed his catch in Knudson Cove in the early twentieth century, who had told Snapper's family about the tradition. Eton was a Tsimshian from Metlakatla, Alaska, on Annette Island, a member of a family who were among the original settlers migrating from a village also called Metlakatla, in British Columbia. He was the last of his generation to set up a fish camp in the cove. He would pitch a wall tent on a platform and stay all summer.

The Eton family also picked beach greens and berries in the spring and summer. Mary Carson, Snapper's sister, played with Eton's granddaughter, and he occasionally took the children fishing with him, explaining that the laughter of little girls attracts king salmon.

Eton told Snapper's father, Lawrence "Kit" Carson, that the Natives had stored their fire in the burned-out cedars. Kit told his son, and Snapper in turn told me on that memorable June day.

Storing fire in a tree was just about the most counterintuitive idea I had ever heard in this damp and dripping forestscape.

I knew that Natives would chop into the red cedar's heart for at least a couple of reasons: to find out whether the tree was suitable for a canoe, or to determine whether the wood was ready for harvesting planks. I learned from U.S. Forest Service geologist Jim Baichtal that the Haida people of Haida Gwaii, British Columbia, also set fire to the bases of trees, fires that burned into the trees' cores. If smoke came out of the trees at any point above, they knew the trees must be hollow and unsuitable for house beams, canoes, and totem poles.

To fell a large cedar, Natives packed wet mud at chest height around the trunk. They piled wood around the base of the tree and set it alight. The fire was maintained until the tree was weakened and fell. If the tree was meant to be fashioned into a canoe, the cedar would have to fall on a slide path to salt water or be taken down near the shore, preferably near a cliff,

Fire Storage

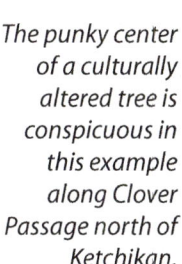

The punky center of a culturally altered tree is conspicuous in this example along Clover Passage north of Ketchikan.

so it could be easily launched after village craftsmen burned and shaped the hold and the hull. The felled cedar could also be floated to a beach on a high tide and secured near a village or campsite. As the tide receded, the heavy side of the tree would naturally suggest keel position. An ideal canoe tree had to be a perfect tree, perfectly located. An interesting hazard of a cedar canoe made from such straight-grained cedar was that, if a heavy sea hit it or if it was driven onto a drifting log, there was a chance it would split in two like a cedar shake.

If the cedar was straight-grained and clear of limbs for a generous length, the tree was ideal for "popping" planks. The bark would be removed and woven for garments and baskets, and wedges were inserted to split planks from the massive trunk. The process was like hand-splitting cedar shakes with a shake froe tool, only on a grand scale.

There was apparently one other reason to explore the inner structure of a red cedar tree. If it was not a good canoe log, it was tested for its suitability for fire storage. The heart of a cedar forms from a sapling that hasn't developed the strength and endurance for which the cedar is known. As the sapling grows, thick layers of sapwood and bark grow on its exterior, and the sensitive sapling becomes the heart in the center of the trunk. When one cuts into a cedar to the middle, one often finds the "punky," or dusty, heart. This product is also called "trapper's moss" because old-timers sprinkled it on their steel traps to keep them from freezing open.

This naturally dry substance can also be found in the outer bark of old-growth cedar and is used as a natural fire starter. When ignited, the heart of the cedar will smolder, storing the fire. One could go to the tree, gather smoldering coals in a fire carrier and return to the hearth with heat. In the wet and cold seasons in the Tongass rain forest, travelers and village residents would want to be warm and dry, and the technology of fire-keeping was integral to the maintenance of winter homes and summer camps of this widely traveled people.

There is a section of coast on the Cleveland Peninsula, just northwest of Ketchikan, where there was a fire tree every quarter mile, perhaps accommodating travelers in the past, in the way that gas and charging stations accommodate modern motorists.

But how did it keep burning? I wondered. Some fires will smolder for weeks, of course—we see this in the aftermath of forest fires—but it seemed to me that to maintain an element so important to society, villages would require a fire tender. Perhaps this duty was assigned to a well-regarded tribal member, maybe to a wounded veteran or a high-status slave.

Later, exploring forests in Southeastern Alaska, I found several other puzzling aspects of fire trees. South of Ketchikan, I came upon a very old cedar that had grown to maturity as a fire tree and had a huge "room" that had burned toward the outer bark for scores of years. The tree had died and was

Fire Storage

***Fire tender**—The author's conception of a villager tasked with maintaining the life-giving flame in a fire tree.*

returning to the earth. The top was gone and all that remained was a huge hollow charcoal-paneled stump with a chopped-out opening in the back that I could not figure out. Based on my research and the size of the trunk, I guessed the tree to be eight hundred to a thousand years old, and I named it South Tree, because the cutout notch faced south. It was the first evidence of intentional notching I'd seen, but I would discover that all the fire trees in Southeastern Alaska had this feature. It was a purposeful technology.

At the same location, I found another tree with a thick scar where its bark had been removed, perhaps two hundred years ago. This cedar was alive and showed no signs of burning except at the bottom of the altered area. Only when I went

Fire Trees

The Asking Totem on Duke Island, Alaska.
"Only when I went back into the studio to do drawings from photographs ... did I discover that the scar ... was a carved totemic image."

back into the studio to do drawings from photographs that I had taken did I discover that the scar on the living tree was a carved totemic image. It was weathered beyond immediate recognition, but it was there, nonetheless.

Fire Storage

The author's rendering of the Asking Totem.

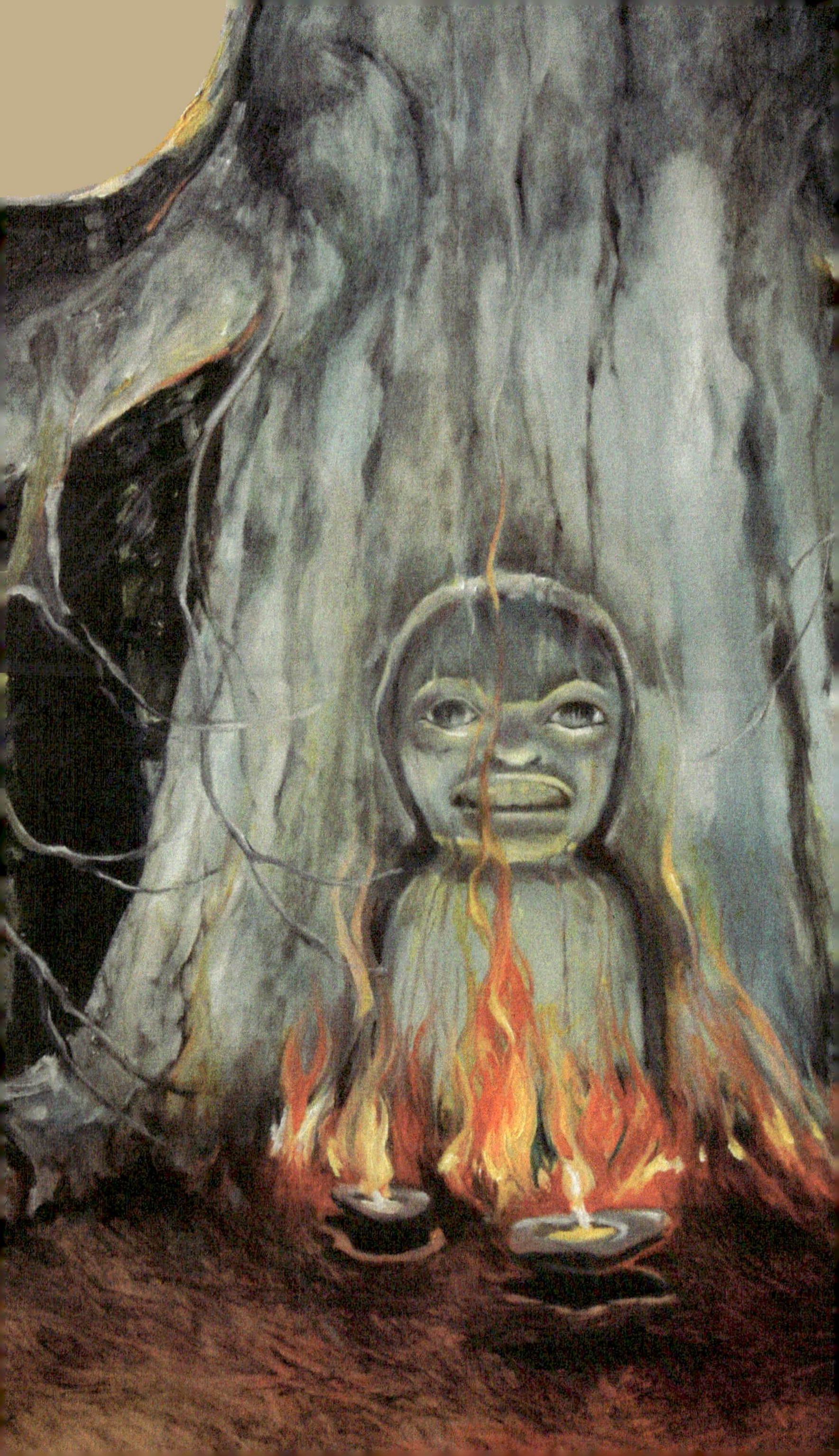

CHAPTER THREE

The Art of Investigating Fire Trees

began my investigation of fire trees as a reporter would: by interviewing elders and exploring local forests. However, I am first an artist and I live very close to the land, so I also yielded to the inner voice of artistic creative thinking—not recommended for more-scientific disciplines.

The totemic image I had found on a fire tree told me someone had asked the spirit of the tree permission to carve into it and to burn it. This tree "talked" to me through my drawings, and, although I might have romanticized the experience, I reached some interesting conclusions. This tree did not die. Its fire was not long tended, and the cedar continued to grow, creating the scar and leaving me to wonder

Fire Totem, *the first painting in a series of five that artistically and intuitively recover the meaning of Alaska Natives' ancient fire trees.*

why it did not become an established fire tree. After doing a series of drawings, I did five oil paintings of its imagined history as an unfulfilled fire tree.

The first painting, *Fire Totem*, depicts a fresh carving with a solar eclipse finding its way into the branches of the tree; stone fire carriers float around its roots. When I bought my little cabin north of Ketchikan, I was told about some stone lamps found south of the site. According to the experts, they were made by heating rocks in a fire and dropping cold water in their centers, which shattered the surface and made it easy to scoop out a receptacle for oil. However, the oil lamps I had seen in museums and in photographs had deep reservoirs for fuel and wicks. The hollowed rocks found near my cabin did not have deep reservoirs, and I came to realize they were fire carriers. Everyone must have had one. They were probably part of the kit one carried, as a person carries a disposable lighter or waterproof matches today.

Ancient stone fire carriers in the author's collection hold new flame.

My second painting, *Winter Solstice*, features the cold, flat light of deep winter and disturbed snow on bare salmonberry branches. The snow in front of the tree is imprinted by moccasins and wolf paws, and behind the tree a low, pale sun

Winter Solstice *imagines a fire tree cradling life-giving warmth in the midst of a chlll Alaskan winter.*

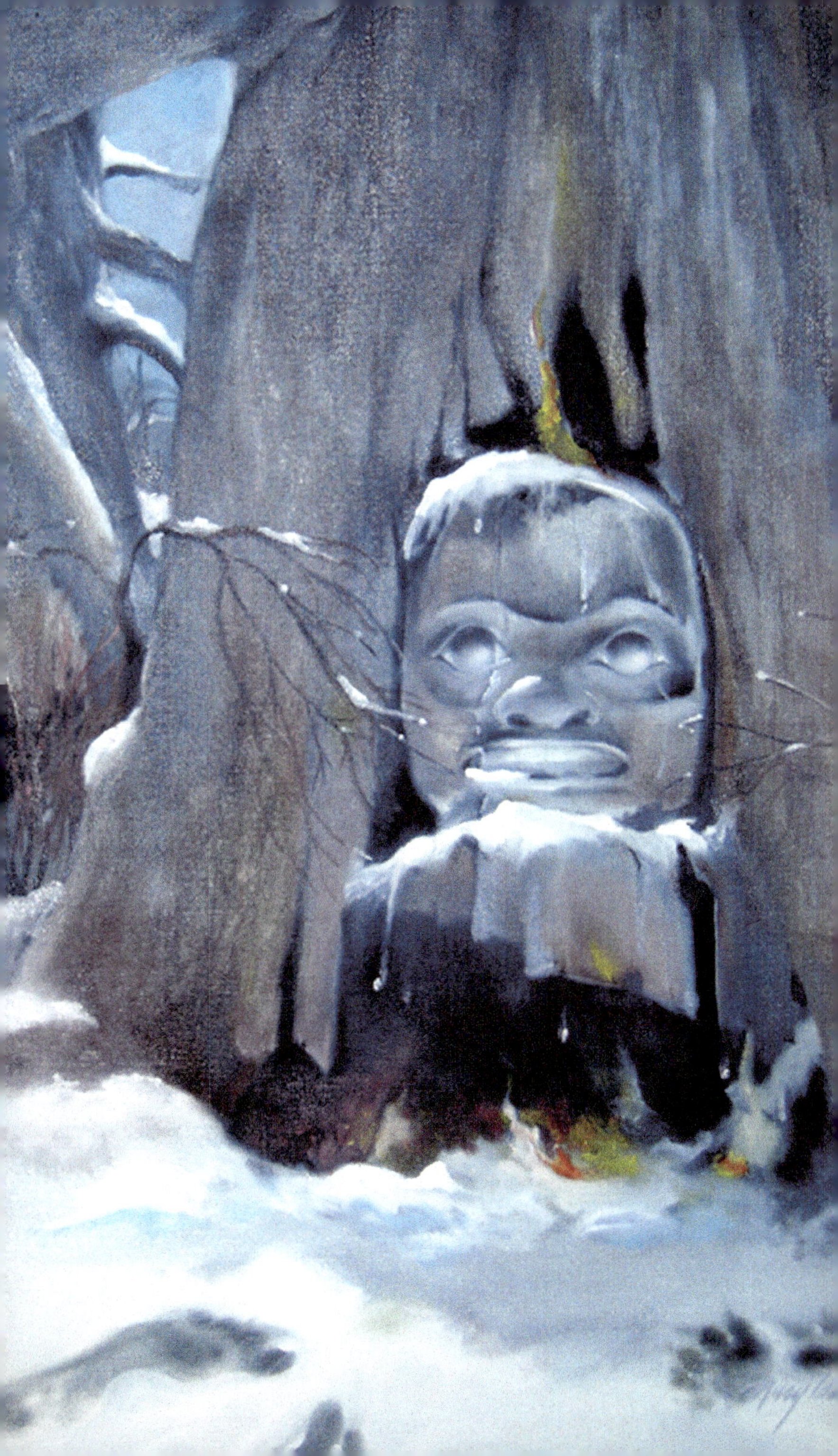

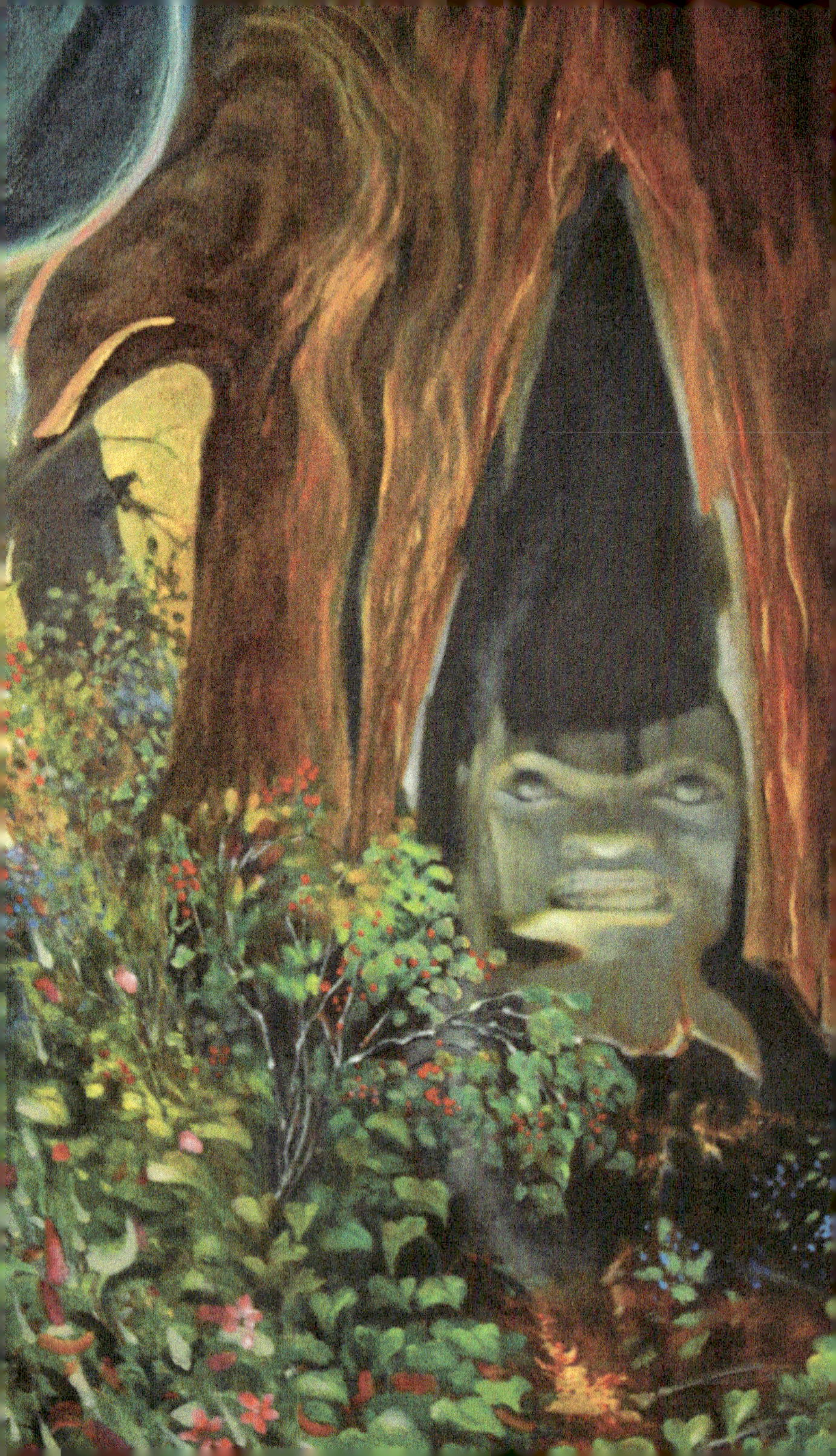

sets in the southwest. The use of a fire tree would have been convenient and desirable for comfort in winter.

In the third painting, *Summer Comet*, the totem is further burned away; only its face is visible in summer bloom. The tree is hidden in the crush of the rain forest's growth and abundance. The villagers are at the summer camp putting up fish and berries for winter. In my interpretation, the tree acts as a watchman for the village. Also within the clutter of growth is an image of Comet McNaught, which was visible in Ketchikan in January 2007 while I was completing the painting. I included it as a "diary" entry, but it also made me remember that people have long believed that comets bring change. Every culture wonders about a surprise entry in the sky. In this painting, the comet portends the coming of smallpox and other deadly diseases.

The fourth painting, *Comet Totem*, shows a comet streaking through the ghost totem over Orion's belt in the nineteenth century, when smallpox and measles epidemics raged, killing more than eighty percent of Alaska Natives. A once-powerful shaman, originally crowned by a frenzy of long, black locks, is reduced to a shadow, dancing with a bundle of fire. He is covered with red spots and he is bald. His great tangle of hair is gone, symbolizing a defenseless people killed by foreign diseases.

These first four paintings in the series were inspired by the scarred, totemic image I had drawn. The smoldering fire changed the carved image through the seasons, so this quartet became a story of time. The celestial inclusions were part of

Summer Comet *places the watchful spirit of a fire tree into summer's abundance in Tongass forest.*

an artistic interpretation and "happened" to find their places within the images, as concepts do, and would later prompt ideas about another aspect of the fire trees. Ultimately, it is the near extinction of the Native peoples due to illness that caused the fire to die, because people were not there to tend it.

While some indigenous cultures had no language for the future, the early Native people of Southeastern Alaska planned ahead. It was their tradition to prepare for future generations, as the planting of seedlings for later use as fire trees indicates. The knowledge of stored fire was to go up in smoke as Alaska Native survivors of Western colonization were introduced to new technologies, such as ready-strike matches. Inventions that replaced the fire trees were far more convenient, and old knowledge was thereafter kept close to the heart by fewer and fewer elders. Eventually, only the totem tree carving survived to tell a story of loss. Thankfully, that was not the last chapter.

My quartet of paintings clarified my thinking on fire trees. All fire trees have identical characteristics, differing only in location, which suggests special usage. If the tree is on the top of a cliff, the top of an island, or a point of land well above sea level, it could be an initiation site or, more likely, a navigation aid. If the tree is set just back from a sandy beach, and the beach is littered with fire carriers, it is probably a hearth tree for community use.

My final painting of the Totem Tree Cycle is *Laser Forest*. I painted every aspect of the fire trees that I could imagine: as a fire storage system, as a navigational system—and in other

Life and light become ghastly elegy in Comet Totem, *an image of Alaska Native culture ravaged by disease in the nineteenth century.*

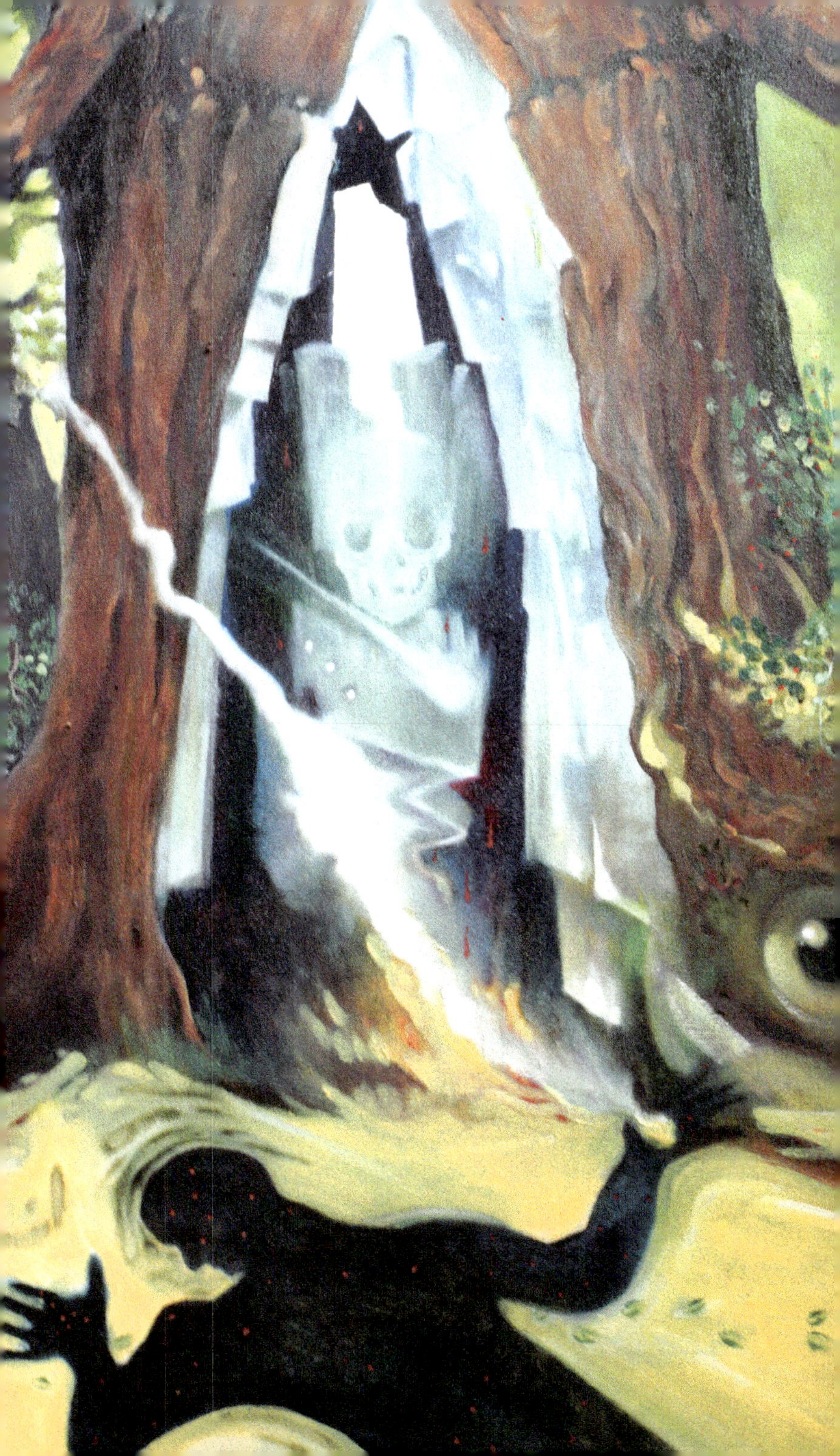

roles that I will describe later in this text. Most of the details involve artistic imagination.

Sometimes, imagination can prove quite useful in untangling real-world puzzles.

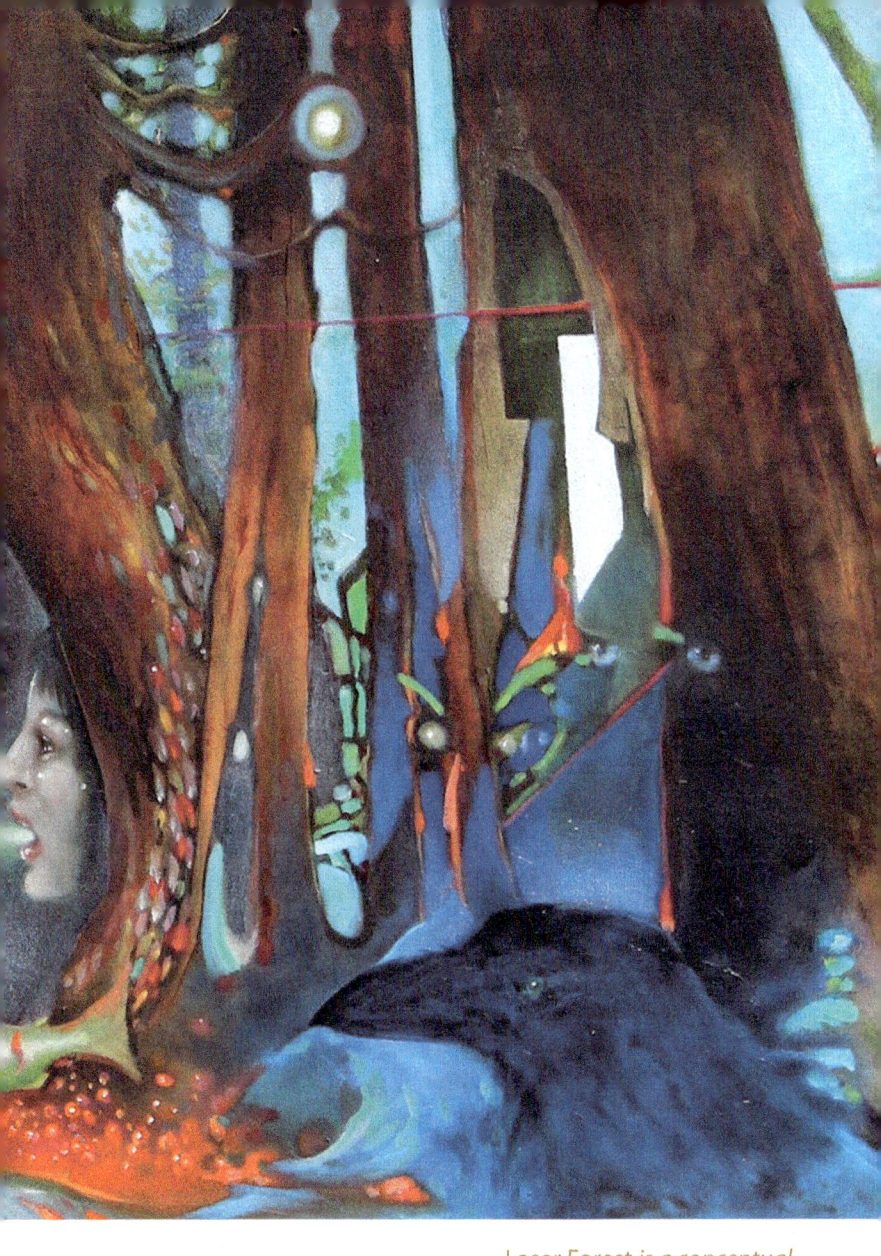

Laser Forest *is a conceptual map of life, fire and the forest spirit—artistic vision taking over from artifact, human memory and research.*

Fire Trees

This fire tree stands high on the hillside near the author's cabin.

CHAPTER FOUR

Lighthouses and Signal Trees

My neighbor, **Dorney Mullins**, was out hunting one fall and found three burned-out cedar trees next to each other one hundred eighty feet above Clarence Strait on Gravina Island. I had heard that a wildfire burned through that area in June 1905, but the resulting scorched trees are different from fire trees, which burn from the inside out. Dorney's trees were fire trees, located so far above sea level that I suspected they had been lighthouses.

That site on Gravina Island projects into a body of water reaching toward Dixon Entrance and the Gulf of Alaska in the North Pacific Ocean. One can imagine Haida Gwaii, also known as the Queen Charlotte Islands, just over the horizon in Canada. This is an obvious spot for a navigational aid, giving light to seafarers in the dark of night or a smoke signal during daylight hours.

Early mariners crossing Dixon Entrance by canoe from

Fire Trees

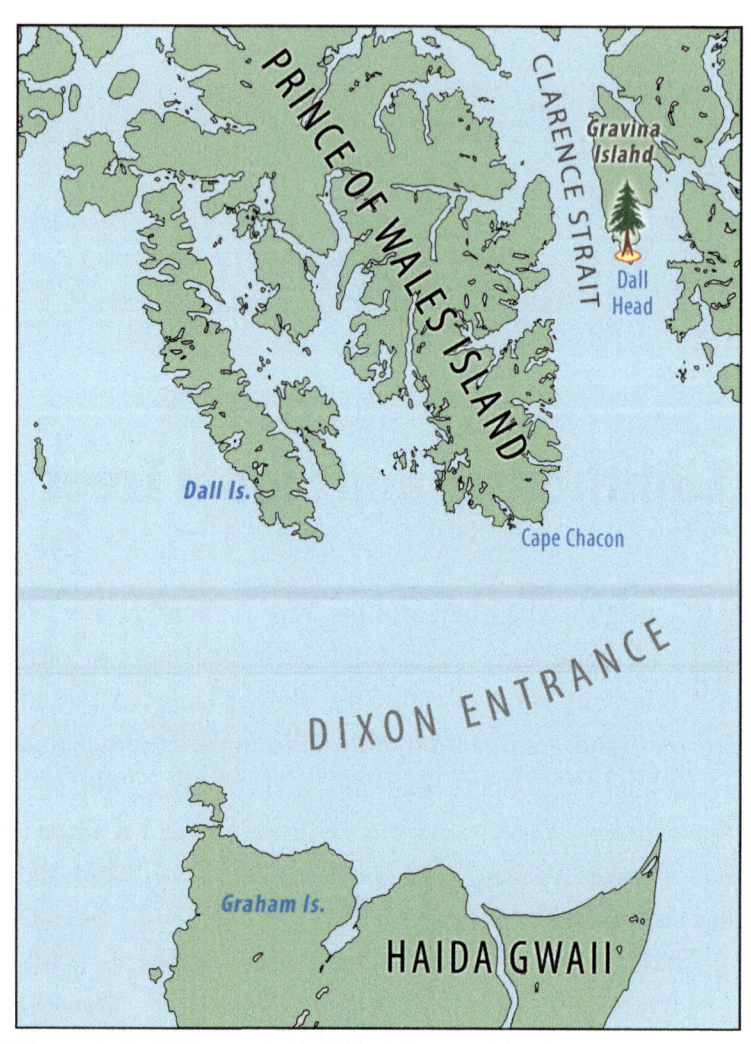

The expanse of open water in Dixon Entrance could be perilous for Alaska Natives traveling in open wooden canoes. Wouldn't a northbound, nighttime crossing from Haida Gwaii be safer and surer with a fire in sight—say, a fire tree at Dall Head on south Gravina Island?

Lighthouses and Signal Trees

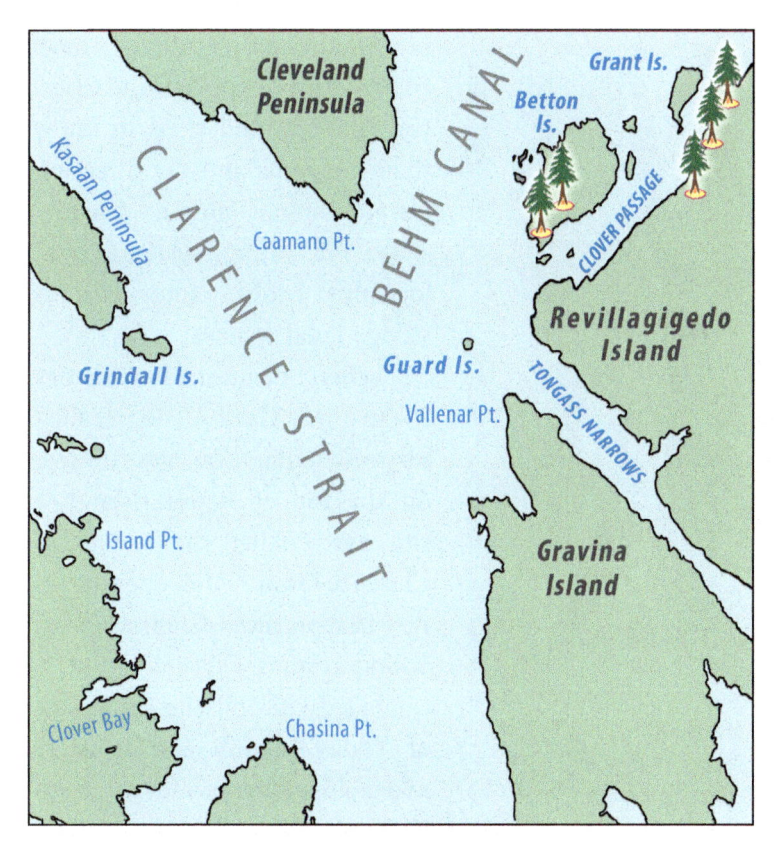

The cataloged fire tree in the heights of Betton Island could have been visible to long-ago seafarers paddling across Clarence Strait. Other fire trees along shorelines inspire consideration of their possible dual uses as fire caches and navigation aids.

Haida Gwaii, for example, would travel day and night. Even if experienced captains and navigators took advantage of the tides and currents, they could still be on the high seas after dark. Also, consider that spring and autumn weather can produce full-blown gales within twenty minutes of the first riffles on the water. Winter storms can give as little as ten minutes' warning, and the somewhat-unfriendly shores

Fire Trees

of Southeastern Alaska have rocky and exposed beaches. Navigators would need to know their positions and the direction toward home or a friendly shore. Fire storage systems could logically evolve into various navigational systems.

When I mentioned my theory to Snapper Carson, he recalled his son's telling him of a fire tree on the top of Betton Island, a site overlooking the waters of Clarence Strait. The opening of this beacon faces Cholmondeley Sound toward Chasina Point, a cataloged cultural site on Prince of Wales Island's east coast. I asked elder Charles DeWitt, from Kake and Wrangell, about these trees, and he mentioned private signals with lights that could be directed toward specific areas. That reminded me of the three closely spaced trees with fire chambers that Dorney Mullins discovered on Gravina Island—trees that could have been such a private operation. I had earlier concluded they could be lighthouses because of their location on the point.

Mindful of Betton Island and of Dorney Mullins' discovery of three burned cedars, I began to note other signal trees,

Watercolor artist Marilyn Lee found a fire tree at Settlers Cove State Park and saw through it—quite literally—to depict its charred heart and the sun-blessed vent on its back side. COURTESY OF MARILYN LEE

Lighthouses and Signal Trees

Snapper and Judy Carson revisit a fire tree that he discovered on Betton Island decades ago. The opening faces Clarence Strait and the east side of Prince of Wales Island. Note the hand-hewn marking above the entrance to the chamber.

Fire Trees

each with a unique location that was significant. Dennis Diamond found a grove that pointed across Behm Canal, north of Ketchikan, toward a known culturally significant area in Port Stewart. I found beacon-like fire trees on Duke Island facing Canada. Artist Marilyn Lee told me of a fire tree on a hill at Settlers Cove State Park, on North Tongass Highway near Ketchikan. Becky Bentley, an assistant ranger at the park (as well as a horticulturist, arborist, and climber) reminded me of the burned-out cedar on the trail at the park.

The locations of signal fire trees seemed to have everything to do with navigation and communication. Some were positioned on what is now

This tall fire tree on Heceta Island has access opening out to Old Harbor in Sea Otter Sound, off of northwest Prince of Wales Island.
PHOTO BY JIM BAICHTAL

Lighthouses and Signal Trees

private property or sensitive sites, making it unethical to divulge locations. But when Assistant Ranger Bentley told me of the huge fire tree at Settlers Cove State Park, I knew I could conclude my research with the story of my visit.

Quest for fire—*The author examines a fire-altered tree on Heceta Island. Behind the small opening at the front of this ancient red cedar (photo at right), one can see amber sunlight in the back-side vent that ensured fresh air would flow through to fan life-giving flame.*
PHOTOS BY JIM BAICHTAL

Fire Trees

A graphical rendering of fire trees and celestial phenomena shows how Alaska Natives' fire trees might have been integrated with the sun's seasonal travel. DRAWING BY MARY IDA HENRIKSON — COLORING AND LETTERING BY GRACE FREEMAN

CHAPTER FIVE

Settlers Cove State Park

At the upper parking lot at Settlers Cove State Park north of Ketchikan, there is a sign that reads "Hollow Cedar Beach Access Trail." The fire tree for which the beach is named is a monument accompanied by a cedar grove near the trailhead. The tree is thirty-one feet around, and one can walk into the six-by-seven-foot chamber within. It is charcoal-lined and has a vent hole; the outer bark of the tree is marked by bears' claws. I sometimes position a person in the tree to provide a sense of scale. When I photographed my niece, Jami DeWitt, in this cedar, I noticed an adzed, or chopped, opening behind her shoulder. I remembered then that most of

'Hollow' trees enclose the mystery that set the author on a quest.

Cedar trees in a grove at Settlers Cove State Park may be witnesses to Alaska Natives' use of fire trees and a special kind of silviculture.

the trees I explored had openings, and I decided to describe this aspect as "purposeful notching."

My cabin is two miles north of the Hollow Cedar Beach tree and also faces southwest to northwest. Aware of the sun's position relative to my cabin's location and the view through the seasons, I wondered whether the summer solstice sun set in the location of the purposeful notch, toward west northwest—behind Jami's shoulder in the picture I shot. I could not definitively test this because of weather and the trees that had grown up after logging (second-growth trees), but it was definitely in the realm of possibility. Was the opening more than a vent for the fire? Was it an astronomical system? I named the tree Summer Cedar to distinguish it from the other trees I had been cataloging. District Park Ranger Mary Kowalczyk told me of a petroglyph symbolizing sunrays.

Settlers Cove State Park

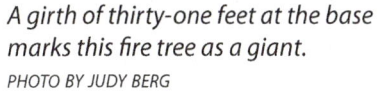

A girth of thirty-one feet at the base marks this fire tree as a giant.
PHOTO BY JUDY BERG

Is the notch at the back an astronomical tool?

The petroglyph supports my theory, though I wish it were conclusive.

Marilyn Lee, my watercolorist friend, mentioned a tree across Lunch Creek that stands high on a hill two hundred feet from the beach at the park; the tree is easily seen after one crosses the bridge over the creek. The majestic tree is twenty-seven feet around and a section is adzed out to open to the east. I named it Herring Cedar because, if my speculation is correct, the spring sun would rise in the notch, announcing the beginning of the spring fish runs. Here in Southeastern Alaska, herring arrive during the spring high tides.

When I painted the Totem Tree series, I included an astronomical aspect to each canvas, which was, perhaps, coaching me to aspects of purposeful notching.

Fire Trees

***Three grows into one**—The author's drawing of the Summer Cedar depicts not a single tree, but three cedars tied together when they were young to create a super-tree suitable for a fire tree.*

After my trip to Settlers Cove State Park, as I drew the Summer Cedar based on photos I had taken, I observed horizontal marks ten to fifteen feet up the tree trunk. Inspecting them closely, I realized this huge cedar was actually three separate trees tied together many decades earlier to create a fire tree for a future generation. The creating of "super" fire

Settlers Cove State Park

Fire trees virtually encircle the author's cabin.

Apparent sun rays in this petroglyph may indicate an interest in astronomical phenomena among Alaska Natives.

Fire Trees

The Spring Tree in Settlers Cove State Park was purposefully notched for exposure on the east side. Erin and Hig McKittrick explored the site while they visited Ketchikan on a tour promoting their book A Long Trek Home, *which recounted a trek from Seattle to the Aleutians.*
PHOTO COURTESY OF GROUND TRUTH TREKKING

trees to be used in the distant future was a concept I had not expected. I knew much about Alaska Natives' subsistence lifestyle and their production of beautiful but practical storage boxes for grease, fish, and clothing. But planning for two hundred years in the future is very different from planning for winter.

This cultivation and tying-together of trees would have spared Natives from having to find a proper tree close to a settlement and from the tedious labor of cutting into the heart of an old-growth cedar. One can imagine the process and ceremony of planting red cedars to be joined later as they grew.

There is a cedar grove next to the upper parking lot at Settlers Cove and in the grove is a mature fire tree with a group of cedars that are nearly the same age. I believe they may have been planted so they could be tied together as fire trees later. The settlement was probably abandoned after Western settlers came and sickness whittled the future of any seventh generation.

The faces haunting this painting helped to move the author toward understanding concepts of migration among Alaska Natives during different natural ages. This fresco was painted on Masonite.

CHAPTER SIX

Maps, Charts and Point of View

ost northern and western Alaska Native peoples were communal and shared their bounty for the survival of all, but the Tlingit, Haida, and Tsimshian clans of Southeastern Alaska were particularly wealthy and food was plentiful.

Clans claimed ownership of resources, which were important enough to be recorded in the families' crests. This wealth was distributed by potlatch and by trade. There is evidence of fish processing in Thorne Bay on the east coast of Prince of Wales Island. There is an obsidian source on Suemez Island off the west-central coast of Prince of Wales Island, and microblades from this source are found at sites on Prince of Wales Island, suggesting trade and commerce. I believe there were canoe builders in Kasaan Bay on the east side of Prince of Wales Island, as there is evidence of unfinished hulls in a

Fire Trees

forest near shore. It's reasonable to assume that there were plank manufacturers, toolmakers, basket makers, and mat weavers who gathered for what we call art and industrial fairs.

Travel for commerce would have been common among tribes of Southeastern Alaska. We know that Alaska Natives also traveled for ceremonial and social gatherings. Frequent warfare—both among local tribes, and against Natives living outside the region in order to capture slaves and bounty—would have produced a need for trustworthy maps and navigational aids.

The author explores a fire tree on the Cleveland Peninsula of the mainland. This red cedar is probably the result of two trees' being tied together. It may mimic a fire tree at Settlers Cove that appears to be three trees purposely tied together. PHOTO BY DANIEL EICHNER

The idea of fire trees as coast markers sparked my imagination for several reasons. I had been interested in drawing maps since I was six years old. Later, I learned from books on Arctic exploration that early Inupiaq maps were more accurate than the maps of nineteenth-century British explorers. So I was prepared when I found what could be interpreted as a marble map buried under years of fallen hemlock needles and live tree roots.

I was making a flower bed close to the beach and intended to plant daffodil bulbs. This bed was

Line of site—*The altered marble slab discovered by chance on the author's beach may be long-ago Alaska Natives' map, pointing with island-hopping lines to fire-tree navigational sites.*

protected from the rain by a graceful, curved young hemlock tree. While digging, I found a Dick Tracy cap gun and a lovely, white marble slab with lines incised on its unique, irregular shape. The closest source of marble is miles away at Shoal Cove in Carroll Inlet northwest of Ketchikan. A second marble source is all the way across Clarence Strait on Prince of Wales Island. So why, I wondered, was this item—shaped somewhat like a thick, marble baseball home plate—important enough to cart from far away to the head of a sloping beach in protected waters? It was far too heavy to have been washed ashore.

Then one evening as I was looking west, down Clover Passage, I saw where the marble map could be pointing.

Fire Trees

The islands north and south were lined up so that my gaze followed a vanishing point through them to a point across Clarence Strait. Joe Island took my eye to Clover Island and then Guard Island on the south "wall." The north wall consists of Betton Island and Pup Island. To the west, the direction toward which the "map" was pointing, were pale blue, snow-covered mountains that hovered in the atmospheric perspective of Prince of Wales Island, leading toward ancient sites. I turned around, and there was *my* fire tree, the first fire tree of which I had ever become aware. A straight line on the map would intersect Guard Island and end in Clover Bay on Prince of Wales Island, just north of Chasina Point. I know of no old village site in Clover Bay, but it is located between known villages, Chasina Point and Old Kasaan. The highest point on the north wall was on Betton Island, where a fire tree is located. All of this was visualized on a home-plate map made of marble. As of this writing, this is imaginative and speculative—and artistically thrilling.

It is well-recorded that early Southeastern Alaska Native people were accomplished Navigators—with a capital "N"—and I've often thought of the Navigator as being akin to a shaman because both of them could "fly"—by which I mean they could visualize the landscape as if from above. An example of a "flight" map exists a few miles north of the Settlers Cove site. There is a coastline in West Behm Canal on Revillagigedo Island named Brow, Nose, and Chin points because, on the charts, it looks like the profile of a man. The Western navigator who named this coast, described by the United States Coast and Geodetic Survey in 1891, could picture the promontory from above as if flying over the point of land—like Leonardo

The conceptual chart of culturally significant sites around Clover Passage is depicted in the author's painting Joe Island. *Fire trees, a remnant marble slab, and islands in this strait resonate with ancient questions.*

Fire Trees

da Vinci, who drew a bird's-eye view of Milan, Italy; and like shamans who fly above the land to bring back answers, and who can conjure magic based on different points of view.

Shamans had special knowledge and training. For example, they could announce the arrival of herring based on the behavior of seagulls flying with the abundance of returning fish, and countless other observations we know little about. Shamans saw the herring with a different point of view than mere mortals. Lives depended on this different point of view. Instead of a New Age metaphysical hobby of shamanism, being able to "fly" was a matter of survival for an ancient culture.

I was working on a large painting, *Prince of Wales Island Chart*, as I thought about maps, and I noticed a relationship between navigation and commerce. Then I painted *Brow, Nose and Chin Points*, and included objects representing stories related to me over the years about the area. I had also winter-fished in the area and once had anchored there in a storm. These paintings led me to craft two more paintings titled *North of This Bay* and *Clover Passage Fire Tree*, inspired by drawings I did of impressions I felt at these remote sites. Sadly, I cannot fly. Instead I relied on Google Maps, which helped my imagination craft a shaman's aerial view.

When I began working on re-imagined charts as paintings, I considered the navigational possibilities for fire trees remote from villages, where fire sources would have been needed to facilitate convenient travel. Because I included landmarks I'd used when traveling these coastlines throughout my life, I saw how these isolated fire trees might have aided navigators in safe passage.

***Points of land, points of view**—Navigators and shamans alike see the world from heights not granted to ordinary people. This painting of Brow, Nose and Chin points on Revillagigedo Island depicts a land- and seascape of wonders beyond the real world.*

I lived in a remote part of Prince of Wales in the early 1970s and traveled back and forth along this coastline, sometimes in less-than-ideal circumstances. It is an exhilarating place and beautiful even in the black waters of winter, with contrasting whitecaps keeping one aware that light and sight are precious. However, I also know too well how quickly the weather

Fire Trees

switches in these waters, how some places are harshly open to the North Pacific and the Gulf of Alaska and their twitchy moods.

For these reasons, I understand how comforting it can be to see signs of other people in the area. I wonder whether the flashing navigational light from the Guard Island lighthouse that often reassured me as I crossed Clarence Strait might have a precedent in a signal of smoke or flame high on a mountainside ages ago. Many of the fire trees we've discovered are located where they would help seamen get their bearings, especially in darkness and shifting fog.

It seems to me that there could be a relationship between fire trees and navigation on what were extremely well-traveled coasts. The fact that my marble map survived the elements reminds me that a wealthy maritime nation would have given the safety of its seamen considerable thought. What an exciting point of departure for future research.

The author's imaginative chart of Prince of Wales Island depicts found items, observations of animal life and the locations of fire trees. An astrolabe for celestial navigation becomes a biohazard sign. Blood-red wake trails a ship carrying explorers, whose contact with Alaska Natives sometimes devastated indigenous people who lacked immunity to common European diseases.

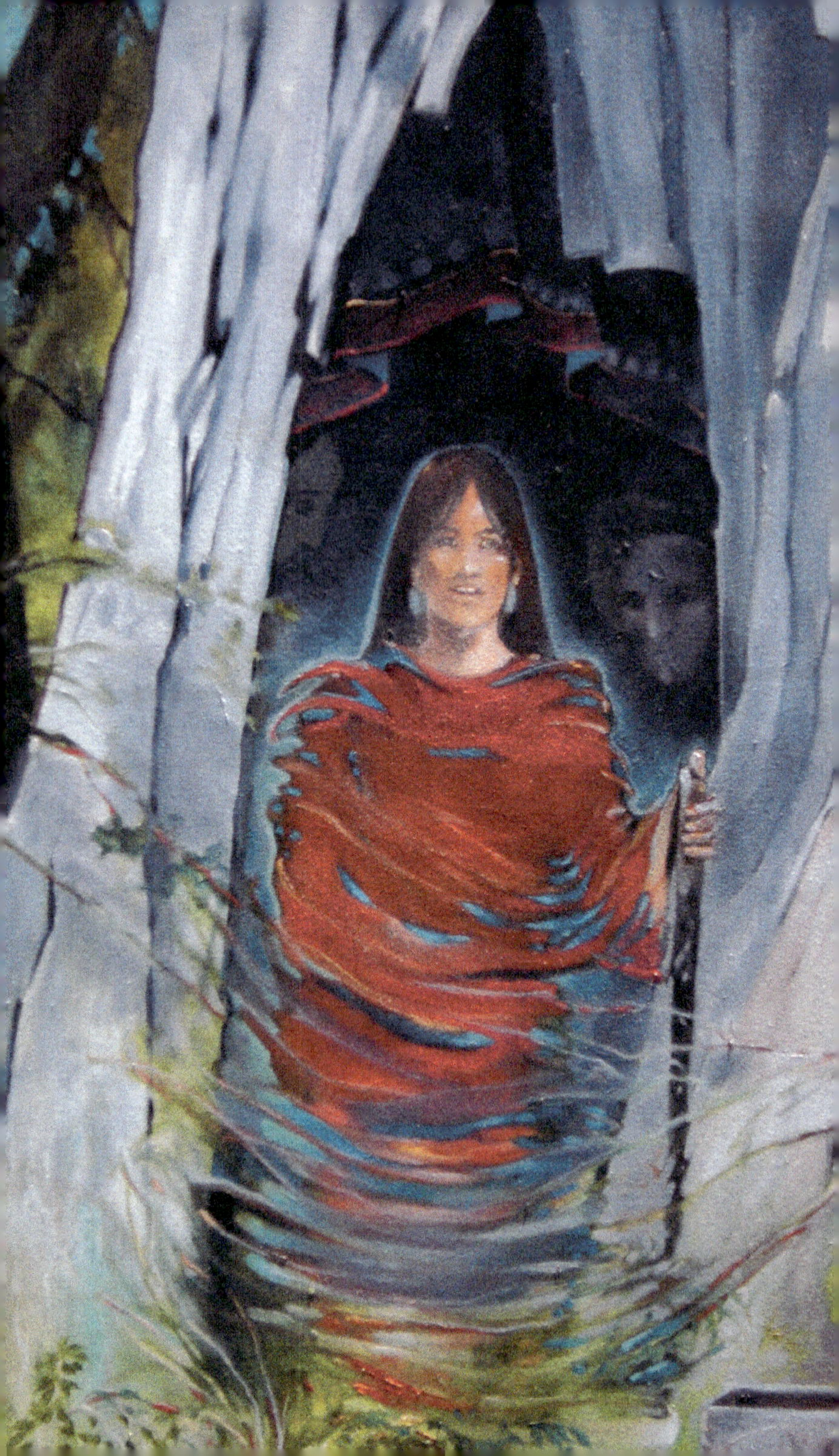

CHAPTER SEVEN

Cooking and Life Celebrations

In interviewing old-timers, I got the idea that fire trees might have been used for cooking, which makes sense because the fire is there and one would not have to smoke up one's living space to prepare a banquet. John Stewart, a boatbuilder who was raised on Gravina Island directly across from Ketchikan, told me that one day as a child he decided to dig into the "floor" of the chamber in a large cedar where he played, and he came upon several layers of clamshells, or a midden. Since his boyhood fort appears to have been a fire tree, one might guess it also served as an oven or steamer.

Also, consider that most of the fire trees have bear claw scratches on the outer bark or in the charcoal; because bears depend on scent to find food, one can imagine a bear going

The use of fire trees in rites of passage is envisioned in the author's painting Maiden's Hut.

into a place stored in its genetic memory where clams were cooked and, not finding a tasty morsel, deciding to mark the tree anyway.

Or perhaps the trees as they burned out had more ceremonial uses. When I first gave a slide presentation on the fire trees at the Southeast Alaska Discovery Center in Ketchikan, an older gentleman came up afterward to tell me his grandmother had warned him as a young man to stay away from the fire trees because they were very powerful. That conversation made me wonder whether their purpose changed after their bark thinned and their fire chambers became big enough for ritual uses. Shamans would spend time fasting and meditating alone in the wilderness to acquire their spirit powers. Relic fire tree could have been refuges.

One of the early trials of becoming a man in the Tlingit tribe was a daily swim in the cold ocean. I have also heard of boys having to thrash their bodies with branches afterward to build their stamina and to strengthen their ability to survive in a harsh environment. These rituals were part of initiation into manhood.

The girls, too, had initiation ceremonies. Might fire trees have played a part here?

We know that when an Alaska Native girl entered puberty, she was sequestered in a "maiden's hut" to begin her initiation into womanhood. It was tradition that she be kept away from the rest of the village and given instructions for the life that lay ahead. When she emerged, she was tattooed and her lip was pierced for a labret—an ornament of stone or bone. I'd read of girls who were consigned to huts so small that there was barely room enough for them to stand. Fully mature fire trees would have been perfect. A candidate for womanhood would have had a fire, a covered door, and a notch through which food could be delivered to her.

We know certain caves were important when ritualistic privacy was required, and it is easy to imagine that fire trees might have provided even more comfortable havens. One can imagine the shaman preparing and meditating there. Would not a hollowed top allow an elevated platform upon which to view the horizon from a different perspective?

CHAPTER EIGHT

Fire Trees Today

Don Chenhall of Ketchikan was surveying for a timber sale in Tongass National Forest on Prince of Wales Island. The time was the early 1980s.

"I was helping a Ketchikan Pulp Co. engineer, Dick Inglis, locate some old mineral claim lines around the old mining site of Dolomi, on the east coast of Prince of Wales Island," Chenhall recalled in an interview.[*]

The two men were in deep forest and high up on a hill.

"It was early November, about ten in the morning, when it commenced snowing, great large flakes that grew thicker until we couldn't see thirty feet. A yarder[†] was working in the distance, and we stumbled along toward the noise until it abruptly shut down. Neither of us had thought to take a compass bearing on the sound."

---

[*] A former mining camp named Dolomite was established at the village of Dolomi in the 1890s and lasted through 1926, according to the Directory of Alaska Place Names published by the U.S. Geological Survey.

[†] Cabled equipment for moving logs and stumps.

Fire Trees Today

The snow got deep fast and weighed down the tree branches, so the men knew they had to find shelter and stay put. They scrambled through the forest until they came upon a little bit of muskeg, or mossy bog, and followed it uphill to a knoll covered with cedars. Chenhall stripped bark from the downhill side of a couple of "leaners" while Inglis looked for shelter.

Chenhall recalled that his buddy yelled out good news: "'Hey, looky here. I got us a hidey-hole.'"

Sure enough, Inglis had found a great, big, hollow cedar with an opening in the root crotch, and the two slid inside on their bellies. Inglis had a tiny flashlight and enough matches to get a little fire going. The blaze was vented perfectly, so they knew the old cedar was hollow to the top.

Their cave was about six feet across and the walls were black, not scorched as if they'd burned, but shellacked black from years of smoke. There was room for the twosome to curl around the fire. Except for a couple of forays for more cedar bark, they stayed in the tree until late afternoon, tending the flames and "telling lies." Just like all the previous occupants, no doubt.

"When it quit snowing, we came out," Chenhall said. "The clouds had lifted and you could see a long way off from our location, a hundred and fifty feet up the hill looking toward Clarence Strait and back into the mountains. We caught sight of a spar tree[‡] and made it to the landing just before full dark."

[‡] A tree at the highest point of a logging operation, trimmed of its branches and used as an anchor for the cable system that pulls felled trees to a landing.

The core is exposed in this partially harvested cedar tree at Red Bay Lake on Prince of Wales Island. Scarring caused by removal of bark and by chopping indicates the tree was culturally altered more than 100 years ago.

CHAPTER NINE

Others Join the Search

W**ord of my quest for fire trees traveled.** I had a literary question and was referred to Gayle Nixon, who worked for the Southeast Alaska Discovery Center in Ketchikan. She was in Washington state when I reached her, but she answered my question and I gratefully began to back out of the phone conversation, not wanting to take any more of her time.

"Wait," she said. "There is something I want to tell you. We found a fire tree!" She went on to tell me she had been on Whidbey Island in Puget Sound near Seattle and had gone hiking with a friend at South Whidbey Island State Park. They came upon a steep trail that led to the beach and made their discovery after they decided to explore the area.

"I told Rick, 'I wish Mary Henrikson could see this,'" she added. In less than an hour, she'd sent a photo of a fire tree that stands nearly 700 miles from the center of my own quest.

Fire Trees

There were other surprising contributions. There is a grove of blazed trees, marked by hatchets or adzes, and a large fire tree, at Red Bay Lake on the north end of Prince of Wales Island, with a very good trail to the site. With a group of four others, I hiked in to the grove because it puzzled U.S. Forest Service geologist Jim Baichtal, who had discovered it. Based on my speculation, there was no reason for the fire tree to be there. It was not on a beach nor on a hill.

Only later would Baichtal learn, through his research on post-glacial rebound and climate change, that these trees were at the edge of an ancient shoreline. This information was backed up by doctoral research by Dr. Risa Carlson.

"The shell in Red Lake at 12-15 foot depth consists of a butter clam dominated deposit with all the usual intertidal suspects," Baichtal wrote after digging a pit and finding a bottomfish ear bone and charcoal. "It dates to 1,250 radio carbon years before present. That means that Red Lake was a saltwater lagoon or a salt chuck until at least that time and only recently has uplifted and become a freshwater lake."

Near the outlet are the remains of a campsite that dates back to 1,520 to 2,230 radiocarbon years before present; early inhabitants subsisted along the banks of the outlet of the salt chuck. That explains why there might have been a village here, but why was there a fire tree three hundred years old?

Upon further reflection, Baichtal found himself on an ancient trail that was relevant before the ocean receded and still mattered three hundred years ago. This natural path from North Prince of Wales Island to El Capitan Pass allowed voyagers to travel a length of the island without going out into the Gulf of Alaska, famous for its mighty weather and weighty

Others Join the Search

Sea level 1,520 to 2,230 radio carbon years before the present is depicted in blue in this illustration of the area around Red Bay Lake. When the sea receded, Red Bay Lake formed. A trail is maintained at this site on north Prince of Wales Island. PHOTO ILLUSTRATION BY JIM BAICHTAL, GEOLOGIST, U.S.F.S.

seas. In addition, it was a shorter route than traveling around Point Baker on the northwest corner of Prince of Wales Island. A knowledgeable navigator, with watercraft stashed at both trailheads, would have had access to a grand array of food and raw materials: salmon, sea otters and more. There are still timeworn blazes on the trees indicating the trail was indeed used in the recent past.

Fire Trees

Winter snow accentuates the coal-black chamber of the author's own fire tree near her cabin on Revilla Island.
PHOTO BY
BECKY BENTLEY

CONCLUSION

So Many Trees, So Little Time

I know there are more fire trees out there in the woods. Since Captain Snapper Carson told me about them, I believe that I have identified their use as navigation, communication and signal trees. In addition, I've found strong indications of other grand uses of purposely altered cedars: for cooking, storage, and possibly in an astronomical system. I believe some cedars were bound together for future use, and still others hint at a more spiritual function.

Because of development on the entire West Coast and storms that ravage the coast of Southeastern Alaska, a lot of the evidence is gone, but the search goes on in earnest for many of us who need an excuse for serious beachcombing.

The Southeastern Alaska Natives were not the only people to employ this technology. I suspect that fire trees existed from Alaska to California. Hollow cedars that were recently noted on islands in Puget Sound in Washington state indicate that there is much more to learn in other cultural contexts. There is also what appears to be a fire tree at Deception Pass along Puget Sound.

Another huge tree stands in Stanley Park in Vancouver, B.C.; the tree is a tourist attraction in the great urban park. Since the site's opening on September 27, 1888, this cedar has been photographed with people posing inside its chamber and, in at least one case, with an automobile backed into its opening. Yet only recently has there been consideration that these trees represent remnants of a much more ancient age and culture.

As Pacific Northwest coasts near urban centers in the U.S. and Canada were developed, usable trees were the first to be harvested, and surrounding fire trees were seldom regarded as important. Yet those that remain have received some consideration. The giant cedar in Stanley Park is even protected by a fence.

Without guessing the uses of fire trees, Forest Service archeologist Dr. Risa Carlson took photographs of these trees in Tongass National Forest while she was conducting a cultural assessment for future timber sales. I asked her why she singled them out, and she said, "They looked important." And indeed they are.

"Pay attention in the woods because great things in nature only happen once," Alaskan pioneer and author Margaret E. Bell once told me. Each cedar tells a different story, and there are many more stories to hear as the wind gives us the cedar's music.

There is still speculation as to why there is no written description of a fire tree by Southeast Alaskan writers and scientists. I asked Louise Clark, a Tlingit of Metlakatla, whether she had ever heard of them, and I told her that I wondered why so few elders knew anything about them. Clark was not surprised. She compared fire trees to Ravenstail Weaving—an ancient style of twining practiced along our Northwest Coast until the late 1700s, when it "slept" for almost two hundred years until it was revived as an art form by Cheryl Samuel through classes and her book, *The Ravens Tail*. §

I recall elder Jonathan DeWitt's mother and sister speaking Tlingit and laughing hysterically, remembering some event from the past that made it into their conversation. It is hard to imagine this much fun disappearing.

So as we go into the woods looking for more adventure and more evidence, let's hope the cedars will continue to talk to us, slowly giving up surprises. Many fire trees still stand to delight my painter's eye and the eyes of knowing descendants of the Alaska Natives who invented them. They can also delight thoughtful scientists—anthropologists and archeologists and naturalists—who are paying attention.

---

§ *University of British Columbia Press, 1987, www.ravenstail.com.*

EPILOGUE

I asked George Pasley of Ketchikan to write a poem about the constructed fire tree at Settlers Cove State Park. He graciously accepted and made a fine tribute.

The Great Hollow Cedar

The great hollow cedar
Whispers, I am not what you see—
A giant in decline
Battered and scarred and torn
Debris at my feet in assorted decay,
Gnarled and curled and uglier than most,
A curiosity to benefit your wonder
Before you pass on.

I am not what you see
I am more than you see
I am what I was, a giant,
Both better and less
I am not what you see, I am what you were and are and will be.

I am lofty ambitions knocked low,
Dreams broken and detoured and broken some more.
Life snatched and abused,
Love lost and tossed
And misunderstood,
Appreciated not—
But found finally again
In the middle of storm.

I am your pride,
Burnt and rekindled
Made humble and faithful
And sent searching at midnight
For those whom the night
Has caught and held hostage by terror.

That's who I am
And here's what I say:
Take shelter in me,
In my scars and my wounds.
There is nothing you see
That I haven't seen
And I am magnificent
Because of it all.

— George Pasley
Ketchikan, Alaska

BIBLIOGRAPHY

Carlson, Risa J. "A Predictive Model for Early Holocene Archaeological Sites in Southeast Alaska based on Elevated Palaeobeaches." Unpublished doctoral dissertation, Cambridge University, 2012.

Krause, Aurel. Translated by Erna Gunther. "The Tlingit Indian: Results of a Trip to the Northwest Coast of America and the Bering Straits." Seattle, University of Washington Press, 1972.

Petrof, Ivan. "Explorations in Alaska." Washington D.C., United States Printing Office, (1880): Population and Resources, etc., of Alaska, 55-284.

Reid, William. Photographs by Adelaide DeMenil. "Out of the Silence." New York, Outerbridges and Dienstfrey, 1971.

Schwatka, Fredrick First Lieutenant. "Third Calvary: Explorations in Alaska." Washington D.C., United States Printing Office, (1883): Introduction and Narrative: 285-296, Description of Indian Tribes, 323-337.

Swanton, John. "Tlingit Myths and Texts." Washington D.C., Government Printing Office, 1909; reprinted: New York, Johnson Reprint Corporation, 1970.

ACKNOWLEDGMENTS

To Lawrence "Snapper" Carson, who told me what a fire tree was. It was such a gift to find a new mystery in the forest, a gift that changed my perspective of history and my life.

To my editorial advisor, Lael Morgan. I needed extreme guidance in the structure of my theories that blended painting, drawing, photography—facts and leaps of logic that needed understanding by someone who knew the specialized history about which I was weaving experience and conjecture. Lael has been writing about different geographical and cultural areas of Alaska since the 1950s. When I was told that I needed an editor for my jerky passages, I thought first of Lael. It took some time to track her down and more time for her to respond to my flight of fancy, but she did, only because it was something about which she had never heard. She succumbed to curiosity.

To Jim Baichtal, Sc.D. (Hon), for believing in me and supporting my discoveries and journey throughout. For directing me to Google Maps to discover why tree locations were deliberate, based on ancient sites and historic camps. He is a scientist, cartographer, woodsman and trailblazer in the literal sense. He is also a teacher who fills auditoriums with lectures on ancient shorelines, glacial rebound and fossil discoveries. You might have seen him on the National Geographic channel discovering an ancient palm leaf on an island in Alaska.

To Becky Bentley, who took me to fire trees she discovered back in the forest, on cliffs, and behind beaches. Becky, an arborist by trade and education, climbs trees with climbing gear. She is a small-boat handler and lives off the grid. She also weaves baskets and hats from cedar bark she harvests herself. She is the first person to ever tell me I am bossy.

To Dennis Diamond for helping me to find cedars that endorsed my theories on lighthouses and fire storage. He works for the United States Coast Guard, is a commercial fisherman, explores historic trails and builds wooden boats—which is why he doesn't have time to put new ribs in my Davis rowing skiff.

To Dr. Risa Carlson, who endorsed my explorations. A woman devoted to her science with a passion, Dr. Carlson told me she is obsessed with obsidian microblades from thousands of years ago. She is able to read the forest to further her research and spends entire seasons in the Tongass sharing her method and tenacity with interns from Alaska and the world. One intern told me she cannot keep up with Risa in the long days of summer. Then there are the bears.

And to Chip Porter for teaching me small-boat handling and adventure. Chip diplomatically told me to get an editor.

ABOUT THE AUTHOR

MARY IDA HENRIKSON is an artist of the Tongass forest, inspired by its spirit, its natural history and the human attempts to conquer it and manage it. Watching the Tongass define itself on these levels requires interactive human processes, from hiking a groomed trail with a guide to exploring like a pioneer. Mary has done both. She has lived remotely and has traveled extensively for work along the Inside Passage of the Tongass. She has also studied the human presence historically and anthropologically.

Mary was born in Ketchikan before the ramped-up timber industry, when it was a fishing town. Her grandfather was a troller in the 1940s and '50s. She began to paint in oil when she was 13. She attended Central Washington University as an undergraduate and received an MFA at Claremont Graduate University. She came home to explore and to apply her education to her art. She taught at the University of Alaska Southeast and in her own Danger Island Studio on Creek Street in Ketchikan. She also taught at Central Washington University, at Columbia Basin College in Washington state, and at Scripps College in California.

Some of Mary's paintings have a human footprint—a passing footfall barely noticed, a remnant. Living in the Tongass for decades has allowed Mary to see a trail change, from a log across a creek to a bridge across a creek, and to see animal trails change into groomed trails. She has found the artifacts of hunters (an old tree stand) and trappers (a handmade snare). She has found coins, a hand foghorn, and ancient camp sites on the beach. All of these discoveries have stories and find vibrant places in her paintings.

PHOTO BY JUDY BERG